THE SEARCH FOR INNER PEACE

By
Dr. Gerald Mann

GERALD MANN MINISTRIES
P.O. BOX 160100
AUSTIN, TX 78716
(800) 974-HOPE (4673)

The Search for Inner Peace
ISBN 0-9678502-0-7

This book, or parts thereof, may not be reproduced in any form without written permission of Gerald Mann Ministries.

Unless otherwise noted, all Scripture references are from the Good News Bible, Today's English Version, second edition, copyright © 1992, Thomas Nelson Publishers, Nashville, TN.

Scripture references marked KJV are from the King James Version of the Bible.

Names are changed on all personal references used in examples unless otherwise noted.

TABLE OF CONTENTS

	Introduction	7
1	Challenging Our Illusions	11
2	Accepting The Truth About God	23
3	Feeling God's Forgiveness	35
4	Giving God's Forgiveness	51
5	Making Matter Matter	67
6	Dissolving Anger	81
7	The Power Of Laughter	97
8	Finding The Will Of God	111
	About The Author	125

"The mountains and hills may crumble, but my love for you will never end; I will keep forever my promise of peace. So says the Lord who loves you."

Isaiah 54:10

INTRODUCTION

This book is not about achieving a detached state of unbrokenness in the midst of a harsh world. I don't have that kind of inner peace. Some do, I suppose…maybe the secluded mystics or those who chemically alter their consciousness. I've had a few experiences with the former approach. I've taken contemplative retreats, fasted, emptied my mind, and narrowed my focus to the spiritual center of life. I recommend it.

But this kind of inner peace is not our subject here. This is a testimony of my search for (not discovery of) the inner peace Jesus promised His disciples during His final hours with them. You can read about it in Luke 19 and John 14. He wept over Jerusalem as He looked down on the city from the Mount of Olives: *"If you only knew today what is needed for peace!"* (Luke 19:42) During His last meal, He told His disciples that they would not be left alone, that He would come back to them. *"Peace is what I leave with you; it is my own peace that I give you.*

I do not give it as the world does." (John 14:27)

What is His peace? It certainly couldn't be serene tranquility or inner harmony, because Jesus didn't display these traits during His final hours. Look at Him in the Garden of Gethsemane (Matthew 26). He is depressed, stressed, and frustrated. He bargains with God to avoid the cross. He scolds His disciples for being clueless. He is no detached, serene superman. He is a sweaty-palmed, inwardly-torn, red-blooded mortal.

The peace He portrays here and the peace He promised to give to us is what I call "Nevertheless Peace." It is the kind which runs the entire gamut of human emotions—fear, bargaining, questioning, fretting—but in the end, says to God, *"Nevertheless, I surrender to Your will."*

Inner peace is self-abandonment to the will of God. C. S. Lewis said that all religious conversions were, in the end, surrenders or capitulations.

So inner peace is not a state of detached serenity which we achieve and maintain. It is a process. That's why the title of this book is about the search for, not the discovery of, inner peace. Abandoning oneself to the will of God is never finished; therefore, inner peace is never fully kept.

When it comes to inner peace, I'm still under construction. What follows here are the journal entries of a pilgrim on his way. Come join me.

Gerald Mann

CHAPTER ONE

CHALLENGING OUR ILLUSIONS

When we speak of abandoning our wills to the will of God, we are really talking about giving up some illusions we hold about ourselves. We all grow up with these false self-images, and as long as we clutch them as reality, there can be no inner peace. This was the situation in the lives of three would-be disciples of Jesus we read about in Luke 9:57-62.

The Illusion Of Grandeur

First is the illusion of grandeur. It is the idea that I can change the whole world. I can be a world-beater. In every one of my commencement ceremonies—from grade school through doctoral graduation—I was told by commencement speakers that I could change the world. "There's a potential president here...a future world-shaker here...if only you can discover it." I was challenged to change the entire world.

If we honestly look at what Jesus taught, however, we see something quite different. For example, in the Luke passage the first man who approached him (Matthew says he was rich, scholarly, and a member of the elite) was saying,

"Let's go change the world."

Jesus told him he was joining the wrong movement, because *"Foxes have holes and birds have nests; but the Son of Man has no place to lie down and rest."* (Luke 9:58)

If you study the life of Christ carefully, you will discover that He did not come to change the entire world in one fell-swoop. He came to change a few people and show them how to cope with this world, get ready for the next, and sow seed which would grow after they were gone.

Read the Gospels carefully and you will see that Jesus did not do everything. He did not attempt to meet every need. He had no false illusions about the world. He addressed the fact that there will always be injustice, and that the poor will always be with us. He talked about the fact that rulers of the world had no idea what He was talking about, and that the religious leaders would not understand Him. He described the world as a broken place. He had no false illusions about changing everything. Mother Teresa once said, "We cannot do great things in this earth. We can only do small things with great love." That's what Jesus did during his three years of ministry. The greatest came posthumously.

I read a story that occurred during the building of St. Patrick's Cathedral. One day the chief bishop went to watch the construction and he asked one of the stone masons, "What are you doing here?"

The stone mason answered, "I don't really know. I just work five days a week taking rocks and sticking them together with mud. Then on the weekends I drink beer and party. The next week I start the same cycle all over again."

The bishop then approached another stone mason and asked him the same question, "What are you doing here?"

"Oh, let me tell you," answered the man excitedly. "I am building one little piece of this great cathedral, and my one little piece is like a link in a chain. It will hold this magnificent building together for a thousand years."

Many of us have this illusion that we can change the entire world. It is an illusion of grandeur. God has not called us to try to change the entire world. He has called us to do small things with great love. I don't know anyone who has inner peace and carries the burden of the whole world on themselves.

The Illusion Of Perfection

The second illusion we must face in order to find inner peace is the illusion of perfection.

When I was growing up, somehow I got the notion that I could keep it all together all of the time. Then I grew out of that, but I decided that I could keep it all together some of the time. Now I have to face the reality that I can't keep it all together any of the time!

I have read the books. I've been to the seminars. I even bought a book the other day entitled, "Beyond Maximization"—it cost me $12! I thought, "How do you go beyond maximization? This must be the new stuff. I'm on the cutting edge!" Later, I said to myself, "There you go again!"

I was like that second man who approached Jesus. He really wanted to follow Him, but he said, *"First, let me go back and bury my father."*

He was saying, "Let me get everything in my life arranged perfectly and I will follow you."

Jesus was harsh in his response, but He was trying to drive home an important truth. "You cannot do it all perfectly. I don't want you to worry about that. I want you to go and proclaim the Gospel."

Jesus did not try to do everything. He came to do one thing—to obey God all the way to the cross and die for the sins of the world. There were many problems He didn't address. He didn't heal everybody on earth. He didn't straighten out the wicked government. Those who are trying to build utopia will find themselves on a treadmill of lunacy.

I received a letter recently from a television viewer named Marge who heard me say I had just turned sixty years old. She wrote to cheer me up. She told me, "You have no idea how much you are going to be worth. You are going to be worth a fortune! You are going to have silver in your hair, gold in your teeth, stones in your kidneys, lead in your feet, and gas on your stomach."

She said that since she turned 80 years old,

she spends every day with five different men. "When I roll over in the morning, Will Power kicks me out of bed, and then I go to see John. After that, Charlie Horse kicks in and then here comes Arthur-itis. We go from joint to joint and when I'm finished with him, you can understand why I am ready to go to bed with Ben Gay."

Marge told me that when she shared this spoof with her pastor, he told her that a lady her age should think more about the hereafter. She replied, "That's all I do—whether I'm in the kitchen, the closet, or the bedroom—I say, 'What am I here after?'"

The reality of getting old—as with many other situations in life—is that you must embrace your limitations and be able to laugh at them like Marge. But we take ourselves too seriously. We live with this illusion of perfection. The fact is, none of us has it all together any of the time. Until we can face up to that, we have no hope for inner peace.

The Illusion Of Immortality

The third illusion we must face if we are to

have inner peace is that we cannot arrive at a permanent, unchanging state of existence and cease having to grow. It's the illusion of immortality...the illusion of not having to die. The last "wanna be" disciple said, *"I will follow you sir, but first let me go and say goodbye to my family."*

Jesus knew that when this man got home, he wouldn't say goodbye to his family because he couldn't let go of his past. That is why Jesus told him that when you begin to plow, you can't be looking over your shoulder. If you don't keep your eyes fixed straight ahead on the furrow, you plow crooked, run over fences, and may end up in a ditch.

What Jesus was saying is that there are periods in life that come to an end, and the unwillingness "to die" to them is what causes us such turmoil. Jesus was always very realistic about His death. He had no illusions about His mortality. He knew He was on His way to death. The cross was ever before Him. He talked to His disciples about it constantly, even though they didn't understand. The last night they were together at dinner, He told them He was going to die and they still didn't catch on. Later, in the Garden of Gethsemane right before His arrest, the disciples slept because they didn't realize what was ahead. Jesus knew He had a purpose. He was driven by that purpose, and He knew that death was part of it. He was convinced that after death, God would raise Him up.

When I was a young minister, I was an associate pastor and on Mondays it was my job to visit patients at the local cancer center. This was back in the 1950's and they didn't have the medical advancements they now have. So almost every person I visited was terminally ill. One day I visited a man who was 78 years old, a widower, and in the final stages of his illness. When I entered the room, I saw the sights and smelled the smells of death and I was paralyzed with fear. Here was a man with only a few hours to live and I was not prepared for it. I just wanted to mumble a prayer, read a scripture, and leave. Mostly, I just sat and looked at the floor.

The man said, "You're frightened, aren't you?"

"Yes, I am," I answered.

"You don't know what to say to me, do you?"

"No, I don't."

He said, "Well, I think it is admirable that you aren't saying anything, so let me say some things to you. When I was born, I came out of a warm, safe place called my mother's womb. I was thrust into a cold world accompanied by a slap on my behind. I left a secure place for a scary place.

"Later on, when I went off to school for the first time, I left the security of my mother's side for another scary place. When I left childhood for puberty, and when I left for college that was frightening. Then I left college for marriage and then I went to work. These were all unsettling moments. Later, my children moved out, my wife died, and I finally retired. These all were even more frightening transitions.

"All of my life has been a series of deaths. But in spite of the fear, I have discovered that every exit is also an entrance. I don't know how much longer I have to live, but that is the way I am viewing my death. Every exit is also an entrance."

This man had no illusions about immortality. He knew he must die, but his hope was that God would resurrect him.

I don't know if I will ever have the kind of harmony and peace for which I yearn, but I do know that the place to start is to get rid of these three illusions:

The illusion of grandeur which urges me to change the whole world. My hope is to do small things with great love, not great things.

The illusion of perfection which tells me that I can keep it all together all of the time, some of the time, or even any of the time.

The illusion of immortality—the belief that I don't have to die and say goodbye to things as they are. I want to be able to face the fact that behind everything that changes in life, there is a God that undergirds it all.

If I can confront these three illusions, I will be well on my way to achieving the inner peace of a surrendered soul.

CHAPTER TWO

ACCEPTING THE TRUTH ABOUT GOD

As we said earlier, the last night that Jesus spent with His disciples on this earth, He made a promise that He would never leave them alone. He promised that He would return to live inside of them in spiritual form and that the evidence of this would be His peace—a calm "surrenderedness" (John 14:1-27).

We discovered in the last chapter that if we are to experience that peace, we must learn to accept the truth about ourselves. But there is more. We must accept the truth about God.

We talk much about God and His attributes. We try to understand His nature intellectually, but we need to understand with our hearts. In three stories in Luke 15, Jesus revealed two important truths about God that no one had felt on the "heart level" before that time. We need to remember the context of Luke 15. Jesus is teaching and most of the people flocking to Him are considered outcasts—the blind, the maimed, the demon possessed, publicans, and sinners. The religious leaders take note of this and don't like it one bit. They start accusing Jesus of associating with a bad crowd. He responds to His critics with three stories.

The Three Stories

The first is about a lost sheep:

"Suppose one of you has a hundred sheep and loses one of them—what do you do? You leave the other ninety-nine sheep in the pasture and go looking for the one that got lost until you find it. When you find it, you are so happy that you put it on your shoulders and carry it back home. Then you call your friends and neighbors together and say to them, 'I am so happy I found my lost sheep. Let us celebrate!' In the same way, I tell you, there will be more joy in heaven over one sinner who repents than over ninety-nine respectable people who do not need to repent." (Luke 15:2-7)

The second story is about a lost coin:

"Or suppose a woman who has ten silver coins loses one of them—what does she do? She lights a lamp, sweeps her house, and looks carefully every-

where until she finds it. When she finds it, she calls her friends and neighbors together, and says to them, 'I am so happy I found the coin I lost. Let us celebrate!' In the same way, I tell you, the angels of God rejoice over one sinner who repents." (Luke 15:8-10)

The third story has come to be known as the story of the prodigal son (Luke 15:11-32).

A man had two sons, the younger of which one day told him, "Father, I want to go and make my mark now. It is dull around here. Give me my inheritance and let me go." He takes his inheritance, in a short time loses everything, and he ends up feeding swine for a farmer. He is so hungry and destitute that he actually desires the pig's food!

He realizes that his father's slaves eat better than that. He comes to himself and he starts back home to his father. While he is still a long way off from the house, his father sees him, runs to him, falls upon his neck, and showers him with kisses. The son says, "Father, I deserve to be a slave. Make me a slave."

The father says, "No, no, no. You shall be a son." Then he tells the servants, "Go get a robe, a ring, and sandals. Kill the fatted calf. We are going to have a party!"

While they are celebrating, the older son—who has stayed home all his life and done everything properly—comes in from the fields and asks, "What is going on in there?"

The servants answers, "Your brother came home and your father is throwing a party to celebrate."

The older son remains outside sulking, and his father comes out to him and begs him to come inside to the party. The son says, "No way! You never even gave me and my friends a goat to celebrate, but now you have killed the fatted calf and you are having a party for this wastrel."

The story ends with the father saying, "Don't you understand? Your brother—who was dead—is now alive again. He was lost, but now he is found. We had to celebrate!"

Even today, in churches throughout our land, people do not understand what Jesus revealed about God in this passage. In order to experience true inner peace, we must accept these remarkable facts:

God Is A God Of Compulsive Affection

The first truth Jesus reveals in these stories is that God has to love us. He doesn't love us because He wants to; He loves us because it is His nature.

There is an old country song entitled, "I Can't Stop Loving You!" It may sound crude, but if God were going to write a song about His feelings toward us, that would be a good title. He can't stop loving us. He doesn't choose to love us. It is the essence of His nature. Look at these three stories.

The shepherd leaves 99 sheep to look for the one lost lamb. He must have them all.

Ninety-nine is not enough! He wants every one. He didn't search until he lost interest; he searched until he found!

The woman who lost the coin turned everything upside down and searched until she found.

The father loved his wayward son, despite the fact he had left home and wasted his inheritance.

God is the kind of God who doesn't stop. He is always after us. Francis Thompson called Him, "the hound of heaven," and wrote a poem about God's pursuit of him. Thompson was a drug addict who lived in the slums of London and was converted because God—the hound of heaven—would not stop chasing him. God can't stop loving us. He is the God of compulsive affection. St. Augustine said, "God, thou hast created us for thyself, and we are restless until we find our rest in thee." There is no way to have peace and run from God. Peace means letting God find us.

I have discovered that one of the reasons I often lack peace is because I have been like that sheep who nibbled himself lost. The sheep wasn't bad. He was just eating a dandelion here, a bit of grass over there, a bite here and there. He kept nibbling after good things until suddenly he realized he was lost. I do that. I've been doing it all my life—not chasing after bad things, but after good things—yet leaving the care of the Shepherd.

I can also identify with the lost coin. It was

valuable, but it wasn't in circulation. It was just lying there, useless, doing nothing.

I can also identify with the young son. I don't think he was a bad guy. I think he was young, idealistic, and wanted to conquer the world. It was hard to live in his dad's shadow and he wanted to go out, actualize himself, and fulfill his potential. So the father let him go. Upon his return, the father doesn't even wait for him to arrive home. He runs to meet him. The boy wants to be a slave, but the father says, "No, you are going to be a son."

The most remarkable words Jesus ever said about the Father were the two verbs He used to describe the Father's reaction to his two sons— ran and begged. He ran to meet the younger one. He begged the older one to join the party.

Do you understand how revolutionary that was? In the time when Jesus told this story, a son who rebelled against his father could be stoned to death. It was a capital offense. It was unthinkable that a father would go in search of a rebellious son or beg a pouting child to come to a party. These were images beyond anything people had ever heard. Nevertheless, that is who God is, and the only way to peace is to realize that God loves you too much to let you be separated from Him and remain comfortable about it.

I came to realize that one of the reasons I am often troubled is not because God is absent from my life, but because He is present. God loves me too much to let me be separated from His will and remain comfortable. The reason so many people are unhappy in this world is because they are not at home with the Father. *"If you only knew today what is needed for peace,"* you would know that God loves you too much to let you be both comfortable and out of His will.

God Is A God Of Compulsive Celebration

The second revolutionary truth revealed in this passage is that God is a God of compulsive celebration. Look at each of the three stories in Luke 15.

When the shepherd finds the lost lamb, he hosts a party.

When the woman finds the coin, she invites her friends to celebrate.

When the father finds his son, he throws a feast.

God is a God who must celebrate. He is a God of joy. He doesn't go around with a stern look waiting for you to commit some sin so He can zap you. He is a God of joy and wants to share it with us.

I've never been able to figure out why church members often have the notion that anything that is fun must be sinful, but it seemed that way when I was growing up. Where did we ever get such a notion?

God is a God of compulsive celebration. The thought was revolutionary! He throws parties! What does this have to do with peace? Look at the elder son in the story of the prodigal son. The elder son is the only one in the group who doesn't understand that the Father is a person of celebration. He reminds me of people I've seen in the church over the years—people who are good, keep all the rules, yet they seem angry about it! They are like the elder son who thought the only way to experience peace is to remain stern and earn God's approval. They miss the whole concept of joy.

Two things happened recently that drove home this point about God being a God of joy. The first was when my wife, Lois, and I were in California and we went to dinner at a Beverly Hills home with people from the Hollywood scene. Several of these people had been through terrible tragedies in their lives, and they began to tell us their stories and those of others they knew. Our hostess finally made the comment, "Beverly Hills is where people think they want to be. There is so much pleasure here, but so little joy."

It made me think—there are so many people in the world who want to be someone else or live someplace else. They want to "make it to Beverly Hills where everything seems wonderful." They don't find joy in being who and where they are. That was the elder son. He didn't find joy in being who he was.

The second thing that drove home this point is in Philip Yancey's book, "What's So Amazing About Grace?" Yancey says it is difficult to define grace, because grace is something that can only be experienced. But he does attempt one definition: "Grace means there is nothing you can ever do to make God love you more than He already does and there is nothing you can ever do to make Him love you less."

A major step to peace is to find joy in who you are and where you are. Who you really are is not only okay with God, it pleases Him. It is not only okay, it is wonderful. You only need to come to feel about yourself the way God feels about you.

Jesus said, *"If you only knew today what is needed for peace."* Peace comes when we accept these two major revelations about God:

He is a God of compulsive affection.

He is a God of compulsive joy.

God not only loves you as you are, He rejoices every time you come home to Him.

CHAPTER THREE

FEELING GOD'S FORGIVENESS

THE SEARCH FOR INNER PEACE

There is no use talking about inner peace unless we deal with the issue of guilt. All normal human beings are guilty.

Let me share a couple of letters with you that illustrate the problem. One is from a young woman named Diane, age 22, a beauty contest winner, life-long church member, virgin, and honor student. She writes:

"I am glad to hear a minister confess that he too is searching for the same kind of peace that I don't have. I have no peace because I am guilty. I don't know what I'm guilty of—I just have this feeling of being unworthy, like I don't measure up or something. I have this hole in my soul. I need to hear God say, 'I love you Diane—I always have, I always will—even though there is not a lot there to love.' How can I hear that voice?"

The second letter comes from Bob, age 78:

"I'm dying with cancer and will soon meet my maker. On the surface, I appear great. I am respected in the church, my family, and the community. Some would say I am a saint. But I have carried a dark, dark secret for over 50 years. I sexually molested my only daughter when she was a child. It only happened one time, but I have never spoken of it to anyone. To make matters worse, she was killed in an accident at the age of 16 and our secret was buried with her. God help me! At times I have even felt relieved because my sin has been covered up. I know I am going to hell. I deserve it, but I still need mercy. If I could only see my daughter one more time and tell her how sorry I am. If I could only have God's forgiveness. Do you think there's any hope for someone like me?"

What we have here are two examples of guilt. False guilt and true guilt. Diane hasn't done anything really bad, but she has been shamed from without—that's false guilt. Bob hasn't measured up to what God created him to be—that's true guilt. But we all experience feelings of guilt, one way or another.

The question is, how can we _feel_ the forgiveness of God? That is a problem that has haunted me all of my life. I think I get a handle on guilt and then it weighs me down again and makes me do all kinds of weird things.

THE SEARCH FOR INNER PEACE

King David—after murder, adultery, and exposure—was struggling with a deep sense of guilt when he prayed the prayer recorded in Psalm 51:1-17. In this great prayer for forgiveness, he models the process of how to deal with guilt. We can summarize this passage by using four simple words: Contrition, candor, conversion, and community. These four words reveal how we can feel God's forgiveness.

Contrition

People who experience forgiveness are people who feel bad enough about what they have done to ask for mercy. There can't be any mercy unless we ask for it, and we can't ask for it unless we feel the pain of our own errors. David is filled with remorse in his prayer. He says, "My sin is ever before me. I must have been conceived and born in sin. Wherever I turn, the gravity of what I have done is weighing and pressing on my soul."

There can be no forgiveness until we accept the fact that we have done something wrong, that we are broken, and that we can't really do anything to correct it. People will tell you that you aren't supposed to feel bad about yourself. For about 50 years now, we have been telling people, "It is wrong to feel bad about yourself."

One time I had the privilege of hosting Dr. Carl Menninger, the dean of American psychiatry, while he was in our city for a speaking engagement. As I was driving him to the airport for his departure I said, "Dr. Menninger, I've been watching you for the last two days and my life has really been changed. I am thinking about resigning the ministry and going back to school to become a psychiatrist."

He said, "We have enough of those. I have been watching you for the past few days as well. You keep doing what you are doing because you can give people something that we 'shrinks' can never give them."

"What is that?" I asked.

He said, "You can introduce them to forgiveness."

"Can't you do that?" I questioned.

"No," he answered, "We 'shrinks' are so afraid to make people feel guilty enough to ask for mercy that we don't ever let them get to the place where they can ask for it."

The first step to forgiveness is contrition—feeling bad enough to ask God for mercy.

Candor

The second step to feeling God's forgiveness is candor. Forgiveness is experienced by people who are brave enough to define the exact nature of what is wrong with them.

King David didn't say, "I've committed a dumb error." He didn't say, "I am a victim of bad PR." He didn't even say, "God forgive me for committing adultery" or "God forgive me for committing murder." He said, *"God I have sinned against you—only against you."* He went to the root cause of his problem, not the symptoms. He didn't deal with the results of his problem, he dealt with the root cause—his own sinful condition, the fact that he had decided to break relationship with the God who made him.

We are created for relationship with God and others. We are not fulfilling the purpose for which we were created when we are out of relationship with God. David knew that. He knew he couldn't do anything about his adultery and murder. He couldn't rewrite history. The only thing he could do something about was his broken relationship with the Father, so he asked God to restore it.

My friend, Loften Hudson, wrote a book entitled, *"Grace Is Not A Blue-eyed Blonde."* He has a chapter on sin entitled, "The Big Sins Of Little Sinners." He says that we all know we are sinners, but we usually think we are "little" sinners. We are not big sinners. He describes how Jesus taught about sin. Jesus never said, "This is what sin is." Instead, He gave us little cameos or video-clips of sin in action...

...He told about a farmer who had a bumper crop and declared, "Now I'll sit back and do nothing for the rest of my life."

...He told of a man who went up to the temple to pray and said, "Oh God, how grateful I am that I am so righteous. I am not like these other sinful people."

...He told the story of a young man who came to his father and said, "I want my inheritance right now—I want out of here! I don't care who I am hurting. Me, my, I, give me, go!"—and he took off for a far country.

Out of these stories, mammoth sins emerge. We all have them. They are typical of our human condition. One is ingratitude—a denial of our indebtedness. We think that we deserve what we have. We worked hard for it. It's ours and we are going to keep it because God wants us to have it as a result of our being so good.

Another mammoth sin is stagnation—not living up to our potential—the refusal to blossom, to grow, and to unfold. Underlying ingratitude and stagnation is our real problem: Closedness—not giving God access into every area of our lives because we fear that we will lose our life instead of gaining. We let God into some places. We call on Him when we need Him, but we keep Him out of other areas.

These are mammoth sins that affect us all. That is why there is no need for us to point our fingers at other people and moralize. That is why Jesus said, "Do not judge, because you will only be judging yourselves." We are all in the same boat. The human condition is that we are all broken, except on different subjects.

Often we talk about the symptoms of our problem but we never get to the real causes.

Candor is admitting that we have broken our relationship with God, and that is why our lives have gone to pieces.

Conversion

The third step to feeling God's forgiveness is conversion. Forgiveness is experienced by people who change their direction—who convert what they are doing to a different way of doing it. Conversion means taking action. Forgiveness happens to people who change directions.

In his prayer in Psalm 51, King David asks for a whole new way of doing life. Listen to his appeals:

"God, give me a new heart." The heart is the seat of all we do. He is saying, "I don't need a little touch of polish, I need a new heart."

He prays, "Give me a new spirit"—a new source of motivation to act.

He prays, "Give me a new joy"—I've forgotten how to enjoy the right things. I'm enjoying all the wrong things.

"Give me a willingness to obey you," he prays. David asked for a whole new way of doing life. Forgiveness comes to those who change directions.

The song, *Amazing Grace,* is a timeless, well-known hymn that penetrates the soul of anyone who sings it. When the rock group, Guns and Roses, appeared in a soccer stadium in England, they took up most of the night. Jesse Norman, the great diva, was scheduled to follow them. When she walked out to do her aria, the crowd was still screaming for Guns and Roses. She began by singing quietly, without instrumentation, the hymn *Amazing Grace.* During the first verse people were shouting, "Give us Guns and Roses." By the time she got to the second verse, everything was quiet. When she got to the third verse, a few began to sing along with her. When she got to the last verse, the whole stadium stood and joined her.

I read a short biography of John Newton, the author of *Amazing Grace.* He was a slave trader who caused a mutiny on his own ship and—some say—threw the captain overboard. He was a slaver trading in human beings. When he was at sea one night, he was caught in a great storm and cried out for God to save him. The ship was spared and Newton became a believer. But he kept trading in slaves. He was actually sitting in a harbor in Africa with a shipload of slaves when he wrote the hymn, *"How Sweet The Name Of Jesus Sounds."* He was listening to the sounds of whiplashes and human wailing while he wrote it, yet he saw no contradiction in what he was doing.

Later, Newton realized that he couldn't live in the grace of God and remain a slave trader. It was then that he quit the slave trade, became a minister, and wrote the great hymn, *Amazing Grace*. Feeling forgiveness requires changing course.

Community

The fourth word that reveals how we can experience God's forgiveness is community. Forgiveness is experienced by people who create a community of forgiveness. For me, the forgiveness of God alone isn't enough. I need to be around other people who have been forgiven by God who will forgive me. I need a community of forgiveness.

In his prayer for forgiveness, King David declares, "If you forgive me, I will use my tragedy to turn others back to You." Don't forget that David's prayer of forgiveness became a hymn to be sung in worship. His plea was sung every time he went to worship from that day forward. He joined a community of forgiveness. I don't know of anyone who experiences forgiveness on a conscious level who isn't involved with a group of forgiving people. That is what the church is all about.

Almost 20 years ago, I set out on an adventure with 60 people when we founded Riverbend Church in Austin, Texas. When we began the church, I asked myself one question: "God, what can we offer people that they can't get anywhere else?"

We couldn't offer them a big building, the best music, or the best moral teaching. (If you want good moral teaching, study the eight-fold path of Buddhism.) We couldn't give the best Bible study. I kept asking myself, "What did we have to offer that people couldn't get anywhere else?"

The answer was the unconditional acceptance of sinners. We call it grace. If you are already together, straight, and just waiting for the train to Heaven, then Riverbend Church is not the place for you. It is a place for broken people who know they are broken. Soon after we founded the church, we went after Baptist drunks. Other churches didn't want Baptist drunks in their church. Baptists didn't even admit to each other that they drank. We went after divorced people who had been "wounded and shot" by their own. We went after people who didn't go anywhere else. We told them, We don't have a lot to offer except we are broken and in the process of mending—welcome to the fellowship of the broken. We don't come here to celebrate our sins. We come to celebrate the forgiveness of God.

I had no idea that there was such a hunger out there for grace, but it was there. When

THE SEARCH FOR INNER PEACE

people ask "What is the secret of Riverbend's growth," I answer: "Getting people to accept God's acceptance of them."

You see, most of us have a subtle kind of pride. We think our sins are too bad for God to forgive them. We think we are more than average, garden-variety sinners. So we refuse to accept God's forgiveness and continue to wallow in our guilt. We humans have a way of turning every good thing into a bad thing—even God's grace. It seldom occurs to us that to refuse to forgive ourselves is to refuse to forgive one whom God has forgiven. God help us!

How do we experience the forgiveness of God?

Contrition: We must feel bad about our brokenness.

Candor: We must be honest about what is really wrong—we have chosen to be separated from God.

Conversion: We must change the way we are doing life.

Community: We must create and be part of a community of forgiveness.

My highest hope for you is that you would experience the forgiveness of God. If you can't, it is not God's fault. If you can't experience it, it is not because God is not trying to forgive you. It is because you are not following the process of letting Him.

No matter what you are doing or what you have done, allow God to come into your life and cleanse you of the real problem—your separation from Him. Become a new person by accepting God's unconditional acceptance.

It is the only way you will ever experience true inner peace.

CHAPTER FOUR

GIVING GOD'S FORGIVENESS

In the last chapter we dealt with one major issue that disturbs our inner peace, that of being able to receive God's forgiveness. In this chapter we will consider another factor that hinders inner peace—perhaps more than anything else—the problem of forgiving other people who wrong us.

When I was 12, I read *Moby Dick*—it's a great fish story. When I got into it I couldn't put it down. Captain Ahab and all the whalers are looking for this mythical great white whale called Moby Dick. When they spot him, they are all afraid of him and only Ahab will go after him. When he tries to harpoon the great whale, his leg gets caught in the line and is severed. As he is recuperating, he becomes obsessed with killing the whale. Upon his recovery, he recruits a new crew and outfit and goes to sea to pursue Moby Dick.

The more Ahab chases the whale, the more he becomes consumed with the fact that he has been maimed by him. At the climax of the story, Ahab harpoons Moby Dick, becomes entangled in the lines of his own harpoon, and he and the entire crew die.

When I finished reading the book, my grandmother asked me, "What did it teach you about good and evil?" I was only 12 years old then, and I thought it was just a good fish story. As the years have gone by, however, the lesson of that classic novel has become clear—the all consuming passion of revenge, the inability of Captain Ahab—being wronged and maimed—to forgive.

Each one of us has been or will be maimed by someone else, and nothing robs us of inner peace like resentment and revenge. If we don't find a way to get rid of it, there is no peace. That is why Jesus was so adamant about forgiving others. Listen to His words:

Then Peter came to Jesus and asked, "Lord, if my brother keeps on sinning against me, how many times do I have to forgive him? Seven times?"

"No, not seven times," answered Jesus, "but seventy times seven, because the Kingdom of heaven is like this. Once there was a king who decided to check on his servants' accounts. He had just

began to do so when one of them was brought in who owed him millions of dollars. The servant did not have enough to pay his debt, so the king ordered him to be sold as a slave, with his wife and his children and all that he had, in order to pay the debt. The servant fell on his knees before the king. 'Be patient with me,' he begged, 'and I will pay you everything!' The king felt sorry for him, so he forgave him the debt and let him go.

"Then the man went out and met one of his fellow servants who owed him a few dollars. He grabbed him and started choking him. 'Pay back what you owe me!' he said. His fellow servant fell down and begged him, 'Be patient with me, and I will pay you back!' But he refused; instead, he had him thrown into jail until he should pay the debt. When the other servants saw what had happened, they were very upset and went to the king and told him everything. So then he called the servant in. 'You

GIVING GOD'S FORGIVENESS

worthless slave!' he said. 'I forgave you the whole amount you owed me, just because you asked me to. You should have had mercy on your fellow servant, just as I had mercy on you.' The king was very angry and he sent the servant to jail to be punished until he should pay back the whole amount."

And Jesus concluded, "That is how my Father in heaven will treat every one of you unless you forgive your brother from your heart." (Matthew 18:21-35)

Now, I've studied the Bible in Greek and Aramaic trying to find a way to change what Jesus said about forgiving others. It cannot be done. There are no loopholes.

Someone once caught the atheist W.C. Fields reading the Bible and asked, "What are you doing?"

"I'm looking for loopholes," he replied.

There are no loopholes in what Jesus taught about forgiveness. He plainly said that if we don't forgive those who maim us, God will not forgive us. This raises a difficult question. Is

God placing a condition on His forgiveness? How can He love us unconditionally and impose this condition? My answer is this: We cannot feel God's forgiveness as long as we refuse to consider forgiving those who hurt us.

Think of God's forgiveness as a radio signal. I can't receive it unless I am tuned in to the right frequency. Refusing to forgive others gets me "off frequency." God's forgiveness is there. I simply can't receive it. When this happens to me, I try to remember these things:

The Best Thing I Can Do For Me Is Forgive

The first thing that I try to remember is that the very best thing I can do for me is forgive. When we are wronged by someone, it can be quite painful. There is usually a wall put up between us and the other person, we are estranged and separated from them. We are not comfortable this way because we were created for community, and the wall of unforgiveness puts us in an emotional prison.

The two most popular responses to hurt are revenge and resentment.

GIVING GOD'S FORGIVENESS

Revenge: Revenge—retaliation—is getting even. I was raised in an environment where I learned the art of getting even. We often talk about revenge lightly. We speak of a sports team wreaking vengeance on their opponent.

When I was a young boy growing up watching the western movies, the good guys always got revenge and we all applauded when the bad guys bled. On a late night TV martial arts show that aired recently the bad guys killed two people. The good guy killed 37! He broke necks, he burned people, he gleefully pushed them off cliffs, ran over them in bull dozers—and I was shouting approval.

Revenge is getting even, but there is one problem with it. It doesn't work. If getting even worked, then the first time that the Serbs retaliated against the Croatians in Yugoslavia during the 1940's, it would have been over. But the Croatians waited 50 years and returned the favor. And it goes on and on. If retaliation worked, the Arabs and Israelis would have made peace a long time ago. Revenge won't work. It never works. You can't get even.

When I was a child, I remember a big bully who took a knife which had been given to me by an actor who played the Cisco Kid. It was like the holy grail to me. This bully took one look at it and threw it in a stream. From that day on, I hated him and I waited for my revenge. Some time later his father died and when I saw him walking down the sidewalk weeping, I leaned out the window and said, "Glad your daddy died." The boy broke down, started crying, and ran into his house. I felt no sense of being even. Instead, I felt a deep sense of loss. I call it my "fall from grace."

Resentment: The other thing we do that hinders forgiveness is resentment. The root meaning of resentment is "to feel again"—over, and over, and over. Resentment makes you rehearse a painful situation every day for the rest of your life. "I was hurt, I'm going to remember it, I'm not going to forget it, I'm going to hold onto it and that's how I'm going to be free!"

Retaliation and resentment—these are the two popular ways we respond to hurt. But Jesus comes along and uses another word: Forgiveness.

The root meaning of that word means "to hurl away." Forgiveness is a word used to describe a prisoner being released from prison and hurling away his chains. He is freed of the things that had bound him. That is the root meaning of the word forgive. We still have people going around saying that revenge and resentment are the best ways to deal with hurt, but Jesus said, "Forgive. Hurl it away." The best thing you can do for yourself is forgive.

Remember Reginald Denny—the truck driver caught in the middle of the Los Angeles riots in the aftermath of the Rodney King verdict? We all watched on live television as he was dragged out of his truck, and beaten senseless. A few days later, he was at the preliminary hearing of the two perpetrators. They were sitting there in court with passive, steely eyes, showing no feeling at all. Reginald Denny broke away from his lawyers—who were trying to stop him—and went over to the two men and said, "I forgive you."

Afterwards, one of the reporters asked Denny, "Why did you do that?"

"It was the only way I could find peace,"

THE SEARCH FOR INNER PEACE

he answered.

"Do you think it made any difference in the minds of the people who beat you up?" asked the reporter.

"I don't know," answered Denny, "and I really don't care. I didn't do it for them. I did it for me."

The best thing you can do for yourself is to hurl away those chains of resentment.

To Change My Enemies, I Must Forgive Them

The second thing I try to remember is that the best thing I can do to change my enemies is to forgive them. That sounds irrational, but you only have two choices when someone hurts you. You must eliminate them or change them.

One of Lincoln's adversaries who had dogged him for years was finally caught in a compromising situation. One of Lincoln's assistants said, "Now, we've got him! We can ruin his career, disgrace him, and get rid of him once and for all!"

But President Lincoln said, "There are two ways to get rid of your enemies. Eliminate them or turn them into friends. See if there is something that this man and I have in common so we can be on the same side." Lincoln made a friend for life.

Joseph's brothers sold him into slavery, he was taken from his family, falsely imprisoned, and at the mercy of the Egyptians. When his brothers finally stand before him, the opportunity comes where he can take revenge. When they beg for forgiveness, however, Joseph begins to cry. He says, "Who am I to play God? I'm not God. I'm one of you."

Forgiveness never occurs until we get on the same side. In the story Jesus told in Matthew 18:21-35, all of the servants were in debt—not just one or two of them. They were all in debt, just as you and I are in debt. We had better not get what we deserve! On judgment day, I want to be very inconspicious. If God wants to let some of you sinners off, that is okay with me. I don't want to smell any burning flesh or hair because it's apt to be mine!

The best way to change other people is to forgive them. If you think that is idealistic or wrong, you should try it. I've been married over 40 years and I'll never forget our wedding day. It was one of the saddest days of my life. I got married just because I was afraid someone else would marry Lois and I thought she was quite pretty. I didn't want to get married, but I didn't want anyone else to have her either. I was 20 years old, immature, I loved me, and me wanted her. I had no concept of what it meant to love another person. It was through her grace and forgiveness that I changed and came to know what love is all about.

Forgiveness is the best thing that I can do to change the people who hurt me.

Forgiving Shows The World That God Lives In Me

The third thing I try to remember is that forgiving is the best thing I can do to show the world that God lives in me. Forgiving is an unnatural act. It is more natural for us to act like animals. Encroach on an animal's territory and it reacts and attacks you. To forgive is unnatural. You may say, "What a wimpy way to approach life!"

GIVING GOD'S FORGIVENESS

The Nazi hunter, Simon Wiesenthal, lost 89 members of his family to Hitler. He tells of being a young architect at age 22, assigned to a military hospital, and wearing the required yellow star of David which marked him as a Jew.

One day, a nurse came and got him and said, "Come with me." He followed her into a darkened room and found a young German officer, completely swathed in bandages, with only his nose and eyes sticking out—with flies swarming around him. Through the gauze, the soldier said, "I burned a house full of Jews. Inside, there was a man with two little children and he covered their faces and leaped out the window trying to save them. I was ordered to shoot them, and I did. I cannot die without receiving the forgiveness of a Jew. Will you forgive me?"

Wiesenthal turned and looked out the window—it was a beautiful sunny day and the birds were chirping. He said, "I stood there a long time, then I turned slowly and I walked out of the room." Later on, Wiesenthal wrote to 32 scholars of all faiths asking if he should have forgiven the German. Only six out of the 32 who responded said that he should have forgiven him.

The haunting question is raised, what would Jesus have said about it? I can tell you that He did say that by showing love and forgiving one another, *"then everyone will know that you are my disciples."* (John 13:35) Morality—acting a certain way—is not the chief evidence that Christ lives in us. The only way to show the world that Christ lives in us is to forgive, to do the unnatural thing. Unless you forgive, you will never be out of the prison of revenge, retaliation, and the cycle of violence. You will never know peace.

Corrie Ten Boom and her sister were placed in a Nazi concentration camp for helping Jews during World War II. Her sister died in the camp. After the war, Corrie went around preaching forgiveness. One day she came face-to-face with the SS officer who had tortured and abused her sister.

He said, "Ya, Corrie. It is good that you preach forgiveness."

He stuck his hand out to shake hers, but she couldn't take his hand. "All I could say was,

God forgive me. I cannot forgive."

At that moment, a great burden was lifted from her soul, and she was suddenly able to take his hand. Only the Spirit of God can bring us to the unnatural act of forgiveness. It is the best witness I know that we are children of God.

You undoubtedly have been, or will be, maimed during your life. You will be insulted and hurt and then you will have a choice to make. You can imprison yourself or you can hurl away the chains of resentment and revenge.

What will you do?

CHAPTER FIVE

MAKING MATTER MATTER

One of the major barriers to experiencing true peace has to do with money. An important issue is the question of how we can achieve financial peace of mind. One of our great enemies is our inability to relate to and be comfortable with money.

The Bible says that the love of money is the root of all evil (1 Timothy 6:10). Money is not evil; it is neutral. It is the love of money that is evil. I would like to add that the lack of money and the loss of money are also the root of much evil—or at least of much pain.

It took me a long time to realize what financial pain really is. The church has not helped much with finding financial peace. Our general idea of financial relief has usually been relieving people of their money! Let me say at the outset, this chapter is not a shakedown! I am not after your money.

We often limit our discussions of money in church to capital financial campaigns and emergency fund raisers. It finally dawned on me one day that I had never dealt with helping people discover Biblical financial peace. The format for financial peace is right there in the Bible!

Before I share it with you, let me first tell you a little about my own personal background so you'll know where I am coming from. I grew up in a wealthy home. Money was everything. It was the measuring stick for most of life. I rebelled against this as an adult by going into a field where there wasn't much money, and my father had a major problem with that.

For a long time, I preached that to have money was a sin and that Jesus wanted everybody to be poor. Yet during church building campaigns, we always appealed to the people who had money.

When I started a new church at the age of 42, I had to moonlight to make a living. I made more money than I ever dreamed I would. Suddenly I had a lot of money and I was overcome with the preoccupation of trying to keep it. Then I lost it all. I went through all of the trauma—first trying to get it, then trying to keep it, then losing it—and at no time did anyone tell me that the formula for financial peace is taught in the Bible.

Jesus gave us some great advice regarding financial peace in Matthew 6:19-33—take time to read this important passage in your Bible.

There are four disciplines in the passage that have helped me a great deal in the area of financial peace.

Defiant Self-Esteem

The first discipline is defiant self-esteem. I find that I must constantly defy the tendency to measure my self-worth by my financial worth. It is a self-esteem problem.

When I was a young minister, I knew a family whose 10 year old daughter was killed in a terrible accident. For an entire year, they didn't go into her room. They left everything just as it was. Then one day they called me and said, "We've been through grief therapy and we need closure on this thing. We need to go into our daughter's room, pack up her things, and put them away. We know that we must get on with our lives. We would like for you to be there with us when we do it."

I went to be with them when they entered the

room to pack up that little girl's things and it was most painful. There were little stuffed animals, little boxes where she kept rocks, autograph books where she kept autographs of movie stars—things of little monetary value, but they were her prized possessions.

For the first time, the weight of what our possessions tell about us hit me. From childhood, we all begin to collect possessions, things that are uniquely and sacredly ours. It often becomes very difficult to separate who we are from what we have. As we grow older, the propaganda escalates. We are told if we go out and accumulate a lot of things, we are somebody. Do you notice what happens when a wealthy person walks into a room? The whole chemistry changes. Have you noticed that when you get a group of men together, fifteen minutes doesn't pass without them talking about what they own. When you get a group of preachers together it won't be five minutes until they are talking about how many people they had in church last week.

There's nothing wrong with having things. Jesus did not teach it was right or wrong to be poor, middle class, or wealthy. It is a falsehood to say that He favored any one group. What He taught is that we must not measure who we are by what we have.

When I hear someone say, "I'm somebody because I have a lot," it has the same effect on me as when I hear someone say, "I am a poor working stiff." There is no such thing as "poor working stiffs." There is no such thing as "blue collar people." There are only extraordinary people. We are not what we have. Until we defy that myth, we will never have financial peace.

Delayed Gratification

The second discipline I have learned to practice is delayed gratification. Most financial pain comes from people surrounding themselves with things they can't afford before they can afford them.

In 1993, the average American household had $38,000 in debt. Now they have $46,000 in debt. The average credit card balance then was $800 and now it is over $1,100. Seventy percent of the American people live from one paycheck to another. We are all functionally broke without our weekly paychecks. Ninety-five percent of first time home buyers let the lender and the broker tell them how much they can afford. This is not an attack on them—the point is that we get into trouble because we are unable to delay gratification. We have bought into the myth, "buy now and pay later."

Delayed gratification is not a popular subject, but the fact is that the philosophy of our Lord, Jesus Christ, is "pay now, enjoy later." He said, "Don't pile up things that rot. Pile up things that last, and then all the stuff will be added."

The inability to delay gratification is a statement about your faith in God. People who cannot pay now and enjoy later have a fundamental problem. They don't believe in later. If you believe in later and if you believe God will be with you in the future, then you can pay now and enjoy later. But if you believe there may not be a later, you must get all you can, and run up the bills and "the devil may care"—in the end, you'll pay!

I remember running up a big debt in the late 70's and 80's. In fact there was a philosophy then, "A dollar borrowed is a dollar earned. A dollar extended is a dollar saved. A dollar paid back is a dollar lost." I learned a hard lesson back then: You always have to pay it back. I thought you could just borrow yourself into eternity.

The inability to delay gratification is a basic statement about our faith. It means we don't believe in later. We only believe in now.

Deliberate Giving

The third discipline is deliberate giving. We are all trained to deliberately get—to plan, premeditate, go to all the seminars, go to school and learn how to practice getting. But nowhere are we taught how to deliberately plan our giving.

We sometimes say, "If we have something left over, we'll give." There's one problem with that. If you spend your life methodically getting without any way of deliberately giving, you lose your humanity. Jesus only called one person a fool. It was the rich farmer who planted a bumper crop, had an all-time windfall, built bigger barns, and said, "I'm going to do nothing for the rest of my life." (Luke 12:16-21)

This man started out a human being, but he ended up a storage bin. Most people think he died that night, but if you read the context properly, the moment he lost his concept of giving, he lost his life.

The problem with deliberate getting without a planned program of giving is that you lose your life. That is why the Bible repeatedly suggests that if you claim to have faith in God, then you need a deliberate plan for giving. Give first to God, save a percentage, and spend the rest.

When I was a young man in Bible college, I once drove the great industrialist R. G. LeTourneau to the airport. I had just been a Christian a few months, Lois and I had a little baby, and we made about $200 a month. While I was driving him to the airport in my well-financed car. He asked me, "How much money do you make?"

"About $200 a month," I answered.

"Do you tithe?," he asked.

"Well, you know my wife takes care of all the expenses," I hedged.

He asked me again, "Do you tithe?"

"I don't really know, " I said.

"Yes, you do," he challenged. "Let me tell you something that will help you. I started out working making 35 cents a day. When I became a Christian I decided that I couldn't be a hypocrite and divide my spiritual life from my material life. I decided to give God the first 10% of everything that came into my hands. I gave him three and one half cents of my 35 cents a day."

Then he said, "Now (this was in 1958) I make $35,000 a day and I give 90% away and live on 10%."

I was thinking, "$3,500 a day—I could get by on that!"

Then he said, "Let me tell you something. It is just as hard for me to give proportionately now as it was in the beginning."

I read an amazing statistic recently. It said that 67% of American Christians who tithe make

$30,000 or less a year. Retirees on pensions give an average of 2.4% of their money to charity every year and people who make $100,000 give only 2.1%.

The difference in giving has nothing to do with the amounts. Jesus never talked about amounts. He talked about freedom. The only way to keep from being enslaved by your stuff is to have a deliberate plan for giving.

I was in Los Angeles a few weeks ago and drove by the magnificent Mormon Temple located downtown. I hear they have several other temples similar to it in the United States. The Mormons insist on tithing. They have learned that deliberate getting must be balanced by deliberate giving.

The church I pastor is a church based on grace. You don't have to give to be accepted. You can drink from the fountain and partake of everything without tithing. Giving is not a condition of membership. You can give nothing and talk as much and vote on policy. But I often think, "What if we had 1,000 families who tithed because they wanted to? For every dollar we spend at our church, we could give one dollar away!"

Divine Dependence

The fourth discipline is what I call divine dependence. All of our financial pain comes from one basic problem: Whom we depend on. We are broken, we are sinners. We worry over money because we are afraid we are alone. We are afraid God will abandon us. I am as guilty as you are of forgetting the fundamental principles of our faith which Jesus revealed in Matthew 6:19-33. We are afraid we are going to be abandoned.

As I approach the autumn of my life, I often find myself thinking, "Who is going to take care of me? What if I can't dress myself or shave?" Am I the only one who thinks about things like that?

Jesus said, "Those are the things the pagans—people who don't have a god—worry about. But you have a Father who will take care of you." Financial peace all comes down to whom you depend on. Whether you have a Father you can trust—and if you do, you'll be free.

Why not sit down this week—as a family—and put your finances in the hands of God and decide to depend on the Father for your finances? Practice these four disciplines which are the keys to financial peace:

Defiant self-esteem

Delayed gratification

Deliberate giving

Divine Dependence

You can be set free from the bondage of financial worry if you dare to take that leap of faith and begin to do what God says to do. The Biblical plan for financial peace will change your life.

CHAPTER SIX

DISSOLVING ANGER

One of the things that results from inner peace is intimate, long-lasting relationships. Genesis talks about how God created the first man and woman, brought them together, and declared, *"That is why a man leaves his father and mother and is united with his wife, and they become one. The man and the woman were both naked, but they were not embarrassed."* (Genesis 2:24-25)

God wants us to have intimate, long-lasting relationships, but the question is how do you maintain such relationships? How do we stay in love?

We preachers are always using superlatives—something is always the best, the worst, the deepest, the farthest—but I'm going to use a superlative anyway. I believe that my task is always to call people to do something great. The deepest hunger of the human soul is a hunger for what people call "at oneness" with another. This "oneness" is a desire for intimacy with God, and with other people.

We all have this hunger to be reunited, and when we "fall" in love, that is what happens. We have this momentary rush of reunion. Genesis calls it becoming one flesh—the two become as one person, so that they are no longer two people but one person.

This is the metaphor used in Genesis when it says that the man and woman were naked and unashamed. They were fully exposed, and yet not afraid. Intimacy is to be fully known, and be fully safe. Relationships that work are built on intimacy. A true mate is someone who knows you as you are—warts, pimples, and all—yet loves you anyway. If you have as many as five of such persons—spouses and friends—you are wealthy.

I won't spend a great deal of time examining intimacy because there is so much about it in books and marriage seminars. I want to talk about what I think is the number one enemy of intimacy, namely, unresolved anger. We talk a lot about falling in love, but not much about staying in love. I think the most difficult thing about staying in love, or maintaining intimacy, is dealing with unresolved anger. I think it is the number one killer of intimacy.

How to deal with unresolved anger? No one ever taught me. Lois and I have been working on this problem for 40 years. What I have to share is gleaned mainly from trial and error. Lois and I are still working on it. This chapter won't give you philosophical or psychological jargon, but some practical things we have done to resolve anger.

Face The Facts About Anger

First, we had to face realistically some basic facts about anger.

Fact number one: Anger is normal and unavoidable. I grew up thinking that to be angry was to be bad. I was told as a child, "Don't be angry!" Were you ever told that? Have you ever told your child, "Don't be angry?" It's like telling them not to breathe.

Anger is normal. It is a God-given early warning system signaling us that we are in trouble. When we are in danger, we get angry. When we are about to lose something we need, we defend it and try to hold on to it. Anger is frustration born out of something being threatened. Anger is God's way of telling us we are about to lose something that is dear to us. You can't avoid being angry. To feel that it is abnormal or sinful is something you must get out of your head.

Fact number two: The most popular ways we deal with anger simply don't work. For instance, you can't swallow it. If you try, it won't digest. You are either going to regurgitate it in the form of rage or internalize it until it makes you ill.

I often ask people, "How do you handle your anger?" Some get this pious look and say, "Oh, well, Jesus is in our hearts and we just don't get angry." The other extreme equates anger with rage—"I tear something up! I let it boil until it explodes, and then...watch out!" That is not anger—that is rage. Swallowing anger will not work. It will come out as rage, you will transfer it to someone else, or you will get sick.

I remember when I first got out of seminary and was pastoring this nice church. I was the young "Dr. Mann," and the building was filled for services three times on Sundays. After I preached one Sunday, we were in the car going out to lunch. My little six year old daughter was in the back seat and she asked, "Daddy, can I have someone over to play today?"

"No, shut up!" I answered. I ordinarily never talked to her that way. She was my number one buddy. Whenever I did talk to her gruffly she would always break into tears.

A little later I heard her whimpering in the back seat and then I heard her whisper to her mother, "What's wrong with Daddy?"

Lois calmly looked over the back seat, glanced back at me, and then answered, "Well, Stacey, your Dad's sermon stunk this morning. He did not prepare for it. He went out and played golf instead. It was a boring sermon. He knows it, the people know it, and God knows it. You and I are just going to have to catch hell for it the rest of the week!" Transference! And we usually transfer our anger to people who can't strike back.

As I said, many people get sick by internalizing their anger. This has been scientifically documented. Quite often I see in relationships what I call the low-level hum. This is when people have been angry with each other for so long that they have stopped fighting, stopped shouting, and there is a boiling, seething animosity just below the surface. You will see a couple come into a restaurant to have dinner and they grunt at each other a few times, and that's all the communication there is.

You can't swallow your anger and forget about it. You must deal with it. When we come to realize that, then we make the second mistake. We use the other technique that won't work—ventilating anger. We were actually taught in the 60's that we should vent our anger. I went to "primal scream" therapy one time. They taught you to scream from your diaphragm. You start from way down inside and just let it gush out. But now we know that there's a problem with venting anger because it creates an endorphin rush which is like a runner's high. You can actually become addicted to anything that creates endorphins. The more you do it, the more you have to do it. You become a raging person, and you trigger the same thing in the people you are mad at. You say things you don't

THE SEARCH FOR INNER PEACE

mean to say, and they can't be taken back. Ventilating anger is addictive, destructive, and it is ineffective in resolving anger.

So What Works?

What does work? I wrote in my journal a silly thing that I hadn't thought of for years until I was writing this chapter. I had been married for six months and I had bought into the whole fairy-tale story about the handsome prince who—after many trials, tribulations, and adventures—married the lowly kitchen maid. It is a beautiful story, and in the end "they live happily ever after."

I bought into that whole deal. I married the most beautiful girl in the class. After six months of marriage I sat down and wrote a sequel to what happened to the prince and the kitchen maid after they got married. It was based on my six months of experience. I skipped the wedding night and went to breakfast the first morning:

"He brought her strawberries and cream. She had never had anything like that. He looked across the table at her

and the cream was dripping off her chin. She was burping regularly because that was the accepted way in her culture of telling him how wonderful the strawberries and cream were. Every time she burped, she thought it was a compliment, but he got more angry each time.

He diverted attention to an impressionistic painting of a castle hanging on the wall. He began to tell her how beautiful it was, how it had great form. She thought that their puppy had had an accident on the canvas. She couldn't relate.

And therein began the accumulation of a whole series of differences. As the months went by, he would criticize her. Her friends would make fun of his tight pants and his prissy talk. His friends would make fun of her clumsiness and inability to dress right. This multiplied and escalated until, when he began to criticize her, she would cry, and they got into what we call the 'love-anger' cycle.

They would be angry, make up, have momentary respites of love, and then be angry again. Then he moved from criticism to shouting. At first she was afraid of that, but finally one day she screwed up the courage to shout back, and they started hollering at each other. Then the shouting escalated to the point where he slapped her. She went into the stable and cried for hours, then came back and found him asleep; whereupon she took the skillet off the wall and rearranged his face."

That was my silly story written just six months into our marriage, but let me tell you something important about that story. It was a revelation of my inward pain, and my inability to deal with anger.

So we began to search for some system for handling anger. I want to share with you four practical things we have learned, using the acronym PRAC—which represents the word practical—which helps me remember these steps.

An Acronym For Anger

P: Permission. It was a wonderful day when we gave each other permission to say, "I am angry," and to say it the moment we felt it. Early detection is everything.

We made an agreement that we could say it without being counterattacked. It is wonderful when you can say, "I'm angry" without the threat of retaliation. Without such permission, when your mate says, "I'm angry at you," then you will say, "Well, I'm angry at you too!" But we gave each other permission to say "I'm angry," the moment we felt it. This does an amazing thing. It stops anger from escalating. It nips it in the bud.

R: Reconstruction. We also agreed to reconstruct the anger event. When did you get angry? Why did you get angry? Were there other things going on in your life? What was said to trigger it?

Step-by-step, you reconstruct the anger event together. We found out that about 90% of the time something was not stated correctly—we said something that sounded different from what we meant. It was misheard. Most of the time when we reconstructed the anger event we discovered that we had no reason to be angry at all.

A: Alliance. We made up our minds that we would form an alliance against the real enemy. What or who is the real enemy in an anger event? The other person is not the enemy. Anger is the enemy. So we decided to form an alliance against anger.

Let me show you how that works. I'm angry at you, but I'm not going to attack and you aren't going to attack me. Instead, we reconstruct the anger event, then you say to the person you are angry at, "I need for you to help me dissolve this anger." Something magical happens when you do that. It is like the sun evaporating the mist in the morning. The anger dissolves and disappears. When you form an alliance against anger, both of you are on the same side, and that is what dissolves anger.

C: Christ. You would expect me to say this because I am a minister, but I'm not saying it because I am a minister. I'm saying it because it is true. Everything I am sharing about dissolving anger won't work unless you have a power that comes to live in you that is beyond your natural capacities.

Whenever I am driven by anger, that is Gerald Mann's ego. Whenever I am driven by Permission, Reconstruction, and Alliance I am driven by the Spirit of Christ. That is what Paul was saying in Ephesians 4. You can't have the power to deal with anger unless you possess a new power within you.

There are many substitutes for intimacy. I preached the material in this chapter in a sermon a few years ago, and one man wrote me a note and said, "I've been married 50 years. My wife is not a Christian, I'm not a Christian, we don't even believe in God, yet we have a wonderful relationship." Through a series of communications with him, I discovered that his "relationship" was actually a truce. He said, "We draw a line. This is my territory, that is hers, and we stay on our sides of the line." Two, well-armed camps! If you step on the line, the sabers start rattling. That is not intimacy.

Then there is a kind of sick, symbiotic relationship that is sometimes called "intimacy" where people feed off of each other's anger. Have you ever listened to people who constantly gouge each other and tear each other down? In the movie, "Who's Afraid Of Virginia Wolfe?" two sick people stay together so they can feed on each other's anger. The entire play is an exercise in fighting, gouging, and dismemberment. George and Martha—two alcoholics—just pick at each other all the time. Whenever the stress becomes unbearable, they have a way of calling a truce. They sing, "Who's afraid of Virginia Wolfe?" At the climax of the play, Martha is boring in on George and he is eating back at her. When he reaches his breaking point and starts singing, "Who's afraid of Virginia Wolfe?" she finally admits, "I am George. I am."

There is another kind of relationship where you do your thing, I do mine, and we stay together for the sake of the marriage, the kids, and convenience. It's cheaper that way and less of a problem. That's not intimacy either. Intimacy with another person only happens when Christ comes to dwell in a relationship. Families who pray together stay together.

I remember once when Lois and I had a big fight which was totally my fault. I was wrong. She said, "I'm angry at you." I said, "Let's talk about it", and we started through our process. It became so painful that after Permission and before we got to Reconstruction, I said, "Let's pray."

She said, "Oh no you don't! I'm not going to let you off that easy. We are going to go through the entire process."

Don't use prayer as a crutch. Use the presence of God as the glue that repairs your relationship.

I don't know what people do who try to love each other without asking the source of all love, our Lord, Jesus Christ, to come into the relationship. Don't try to practice PRA—Permission, Reconstruction, Alliance—unless you are willing to add the C to the process. That's the place to start.

It is perfectly normal to be angry. You can't keep from it. Don't swallow it or internalize it. Don't vent it. Create a process where, by the grace of God, you can dissolve it and experience peace.

CHAPTER SEVEN

THE POWER OF LAUGHTER

The Apostle James wrote to a group of believers who were experiencing great difficulties, *"My friends, consider yourselves fortunate when all kinds of trials come your way, for you know that when your faith succeeds in facing such trials, the result is the ability to endure."* (James 1:2) There is great power in laughter, and it is a vital element in our search for inner peace.

Years ago, I was invited to do a five-day speaking engagement (which we Baptists call a revival) in a little country church. In fact, the nearest thing to a town was a general store that sold everything from feed to soap. Everyday after lunch, all the men of the town would gather around the cracker barrel to drink coffee and trade stories. I ended up joining them there for the five days while I was in town. The owner of the store was a man named Alvin who was one of those sweet saints whom God creates. Everyone loved him, everyone was welcome, and they came and drank his coffee each day.

Alvin had a son about my age, a big guy at 6'4", whose name was Alvin Junior. This young man was mentally challenged, had a low IQ, and was the only child they had. The doctors cautioned them not to have anymore children after his birth. Junior worked at the feed store and while we talked each day, he would walk around the table and every time someone laughed, he would laugh. When they would frown, he would frown. He wanted so much to be included. The men had known him for years and didn't pay much attention to him.

One day when we were all talking, someone mentioned something about a motorcycle. Alvin Junior jumped right into the conversation and said, "My cousin Jimmy Smith has a motorcycle. Last Friday, when I got off work, he drove up on his Harley-Davidson and gave me some goggles and a helmet, I got on behind him, and we took off. We went so fast we passed everybody. We went so fast that the next morning at daylight we were in Honolulu, Hawaii!" Well, everybody just roared and I laughed along with them.

Then I thought, "It must have hurt Alvin Senior that we were all laughing at Junior." So I went back into his office and said, "Alvin, I have an exceptional child also and I want to apologize for laughing at Junior."

"That's okay! I was laughing harder than anybody else," he said. "Junior doesn't even have a cousin named Jimmy Smith, much less one who owns a Harley-Davidson! He does this all the time and I laugh as hard as anybody else. My wife and I believe that God gave us Alvin Jr. to remind us every day of the power of laughter."

What a shame that we have separated religious devotion from laughter. I grew up in a tradition where it was almost a sin to laugh. If they caught you laughing, they thought there must be something evil going on. We have a bunch of "sad sacks" running around the church. The truth is that there should be no sad saints. Jesus surrounded Himself with laughter. What a shame that we have equated humorlessness with devotion to God.

It is true that humor can be negative and destructive in some cases...humor that is used to put someone else down or humor that is used as escapism. Psychiatrists tell me about counseling with people who will crack jokes to keep from dealing with crucial issues. So there are negative forms of humor.

But healthy humor—which I define as the humor we can use to face life's troubles—is what James was talking about when he advised them to laugh when faced with troubles, as it will empower them to endure.

Let me share with you three important facts about the power of laughter.

Laughter Empowers Health

Healthy laughter empowers physical and mental health. Laughter is good for you. Years ago, journalist Norman Cousins had crippling arthritis. The doctors sent him home, he was in constant pain and all he could do was take pain killers. He didn't want to become addicted to the pills, so he started trying an experiment. He loved the Marx Brothers and the Three Stooges. So he began watching them for hours. Their antics never got old to him. He belly-laughed every time he saw them. Finally, he discovered that ten minutes of solid belly-laughing gave him two hours of pain-free sleep.

When he told his doctors about this, they began to experiment and found that when you laugh heartily, your body produces an enzyme that is a natural pain-killer. Today it is universally accepted that laughter is good for you. I read in Psychology Today where they analyzed tears shed in laughter and those shed in grief. The ones shed in laughter produced a chemical that aids the immune system. The others don't. Laughter empowers physical health.

Laughter aids your mental health. Daniel Goldman has a best seller out entitled *"Emotional Intelligence,"* where he talks about an experiment he did with college honor students. He put them in two separate groups with the same creative problem to solve. Ten minutes before the deadline, he gave one group a lot of sad input—scenes of the Holocaust, mayhem, and murder. The other group got jokes. The ones given the humorous input solved the problems 20% faster than those given the sad input. Laughter is good for you mentally.

Laughter is a powerful thing. Proverbs

17:22 says that a laughing heart is good medicine, since a downcast spirit dries up the bones. The Hebrews believed that the bones were like the infrastructure of a building. If they are brittle, the whole house collapses.

The only time I ever talked with Dr. Norman Vincent Peale, he had just celebrated his 90th birthday when I called him—and to my utter surprise—he took my call. He said, "Oh yeah, I know who you are. You are that gray-haired preacher from Austin that takes those calls live on television."

I thought, "Wow! Norman Vincent Peale is watching me on television!"

He said, "I really like your sense of humor."

I asked him, "What is it like to be 90 years old? What do you do every day?"

He said, "Well, every day I make sure that I learn something new. I make sure I go over my grudges and get rid of them, and every day I try to find something to laugh at. Laughter will make you live a long time."

Laughter Empowers Relationships

Laughter empowers your relational health. Laughter helps people get along better. Abraham Maslow was the first psychiatrist in our century to study healthy people in order to formulate his view of human nature. Others studied sick people to arrive at their theories of human nature. Maslow studied what he called "self-actualizing people"—those who have it all together, those who are integrated. He tried to find out what they all had in common. The one thing he discovered was that they all had a keen sense of humor.

Maslow studied their marriage relationships. What made self-actualizing people stay married a long time and enjoy each other? He studied their sexuality, too. He said, "Great sex over a long period of time has to have a sense of humor. In great sex between long-time lovers, laughing is as common as panting." There are many different models of good marriage we can follow, but the one thing they all have in common is an ongoing sense of humor. Humor is good for healthy relationships.

Laughter Empowers Spiritual Health

Let's be honest: If you look at the world objectively, why laugh? I can't find anything to laugh about in AIDS, corruption, war, and hatred.

Think about love. I've been in love with the same woman since I was 13 years old. I was married at 20 and have been married to her for over 40 years. We are both facing the fact that one of us will have to spend some years by ourselves. We are going to lose the people we love, so why love? It's absurd. You're going to lose it. It is going to be painful in the end.

If you look at life realistically, why laugh? I can only think of two reasons to laugh:

Denial: Laughing is a good way to deny the awful realities of life. It is better to laugh than go around crying all the time.

It's a declaration of faith: Laughter expresses our deep confidence that as bad as things are, there is a God underneath it all and behind it all, who wins in the end.

Eugene O'Neil wrote a play called "Lazarus Laughed," which is based on the story of Lazarus whom Jesus raised from the dead. He depicts Lazarus coming out of the tomb. When they unwrap the burial shroud from his head, he is laughing. He looks into the eyes of Jesus and they don't say a word to each other. All Lazarus says is, "Yes." The people try to get him to talk, but all he does is laugh. When they ask him a question, he just laughs and says, "Yes!"

Pretty soon people gather around him and ask, "What is it like on the other side? What's beyond here, Lazarus?" He just keeps laughing.

After awhile, Lazarus finally speaks and says, "What's beyond here? There is only life. There is only the life and laughter of God. I heard the laughter of Jesus in my heart and it said, 'You were born out of the laughter of God and you soon return to the laughter of God. Death is only the fear that is in between.' My heart, being reborn to life began to laugh the laughter of God. There is no death. Death is dead. There is only life. There is only laughter. There is only the laughter of God."

In short order, people begin to gather around Lazarus—people of different creeds, people of different color, people who were formerly enemies—and begin to put aside their animosity. Lazarus begins to attract so many people that the religious authorities are threatened and they accuse him saying, "You are neglecting doctrine. You are doing things that are unorthodox. How dare you laugh and celebrate and not be pure."

It isn't long until word of what is happening filters to Rome, to the Emperor himself, Tiberius, an old man near death and his evil young son who is about to inherit the throne. They summon Lazarus and his followers to Rome, and by the time they get there all of the guards accompanying them are laughing and celebrating. Finally, Tiberius' son realizes that Lazarus is a threat to him. He tells him, "If you don't stop this laughing, I'm going to kill you."

Lazarus says, "You're going to what? There is no death. Death is dead. There is only the laughter of God."

Finally, Tiberius's evil son says, "Even though you are making me laugh, Lazarus, I must kill you in order to prove there is death. If I don't kill you, I can't be Caesar. If there is no death, men will not fear me. There has to be death." So he orders that Lazarus be burned, but no one will ignite the fire. So He gags Lazarus so he can't laugh, sets the fire himself, and as Lazarus is being consumed in the flames, his eyes are still laughing. As the gag burns off, Lazarus is consumed but as his ashes float upward, his laughter can still be heard.

The evil young man cries out, "Oh, Lazarus, forgive me. I forgot. I am only a man. I forgot that death is dead and there is only laughter."

That story is very dear to me because of a personal experience I had many years ago. I've only heard the audible voice of God one time in 40 years of my journey as a Christian. I've had definite thoughts and feelings, but I've only heard God's voice once. It was the day my son was born. He was born early, and the doctors said he would not survive. He was in the intensive care unit and they were trying to get him to breathe. Lois was still under sedation from the delivery.

I had people all around me, but I needed to be alone. I found a bathroom in the hospital with only one door and one toilet and I locked myself in it. I was so angry with God that I actually

THE POWER OF LAUGHTER

began to call Him names and curse Him. I wanted to die. I said, "Take me. Don't take my son. If he dies, I want to die too." I began to call God every kind of name I could think of. I wore myself out screaming at God.

When I finally exhausted myself, I sat quietly with my eyes closed and just sobbed, seething in anger. Then suddenly, way back in the inner recesses of my mind, I heard God's voice. Do you know what He said? He didn't say anything. He just laughed! I knew from His laughter that He was saying, "I am your friend. There is no death. Death is only the fear between being born out of the laughter of God, and returning to the laughter of God."

So my word to you on your quest for inner peace is, "Cheer up!" And as Forest Gump would say, "That's all I have to say about that!"

CHAPTER EIGHT

FINDING THE WILL OF GOD

THE SEARCH FOR INNER PEACE

We can never experience inner peace unless we are in sync with what our Creator meant us to be.

I was around 14 years old when the Baptists in the little town I grew up in announced that they were having a revival meeting. I didn't know what a revival meeting was, but I knew there were a lot of girls at this revival meeting, so I decided I'd go.

One night after the service they had a social time for the young people and the traveling evangelist was there. He was one of these big-haired guys with a red coat and white shoes. One by one he went around the room talking to the young people, and when he finally got to me he pointed his finger right in my face and said, "God has a predetermined plan for your life, and if you don't find it and follow it, you are going to hell!"

This scared me to death, because if God had a predetermined plan for my life and I didn't have any say or choice in the matter, what if I couldn't live up to it? Or worse still, what if He wanted me to do something I didn't want to do?

Then I would be doomed.

The same frustration I felt that night actually carried over into my adult life. I became a minister and I didn't quite fit. But I was afraid to quit. I had the "didn't fit—can't quit" syndrome and I was miserable.

Everything came to a head in 1979 when I wanted to relocate the church I was pastoring, and the members voted it down. When a pastor says he thinks a church ought to relocate, he is also saying he doesn't think it will work where it is. I knew that before long they would be forming a posse and I decided to get out of town ahead of it.

A dear friend let me use his ranch house for three days and I went away for a retreat to seek God's will for the rest of my life. It turned out to be the most liberating three days of my life! I found a peace and a clear vision that I never knew I could have, and it came from studying and restudying Romans 12:1-2. What I discovered is that we don't actually find the will of God. God's will finds us when we develop the basic attitudes Paul talks about in this passage.

The Glad To Know Attitude

God's will finds us when we are eager to know what He wants us to do. Therein lies my problem, and probably yours too. Most of us don't really want to know what God wants us to do because we are afraid that He might want us to do something that we don't want to do. We are suspicious of God's intentions.

Remember the story of Adam and Eve in the Garden of Eden? The serpent appears to Eve and says, "Wow, nice garden!" (That's a lose translation.) "All you can eat, lovely flowers, no mosquitos and bugs to bite on you, and you can eat anything you want."

Eve answered, "Yes, anything but one thing. We can't eat from that tree in the middle of the garden."

"Why not?" the serpent asked.

"Because God told us if we eat of the tree in the middle of the garden we will die."

I can hear the serpent now saying, "Is that what He told you? He is trying to put one over on you! You won't die. He doesn't want you to eat it because if you eat it you will become like

Him." Therein was sown the seed of suspicion. Adam and Eve suspected that God's motives were not in their best interest.

I believe Adam and Eve are symbols of all of us. You and I are like Adam and Eve. We are suspicious that God is not after our best interests. There is only one cure for this and that is to meet God as a God of mercy. That is why Paul says that because of God's great mercy He is appealing to us."

What happened to me in my personal retreat is that for the first time I fully accepted the fact that God is always in my corner, and whatever His will is for me, it is best. God doesn't want to rob me of my dream. What He wants me to do is hitch my dream to His scheme. What is His scheme? It is to reconcile Himself with everybody. God wants to love you. He wants you to be in His family. He wants to bring the whole world to Himself, and He uses people who know about His mercy to reach other people. God doesn't want to take away your dream, He wants you to attach your dream to His scheme. The only dream we should ever give up is one that would obstruct God's love.

Do you really want to know God's will? Do you trust Him enough to know His will? If you are glad to know, God's will will find you.

The Glad To Go Attitude

God's will finds people who are eager to do what He wants them to do. When He calls us, we are glad to go.

God doesn't reveal Himself to tire-kickers. Do you know what a tire-kicker is? It is a phrase used by car salesmen. A tire-kicker is someone who comes on a car lot, walks around and kicks a lot of tires, but doesn't buy anything.

Why would God waste His time revealing His will to us if we aren't going to do it anyway? Most of the time I have a "wait and see" attitude. "God, You tell me what You want me to do, then I will decide if I want to do it." But God doesn't work that way. God doesn't reveal Himself to tire-kickers. He reveals Himself to people who are eager to go.

I read an article by a psychologist who studied the differences between those who are happy in the workplace and those who are unhappy. She said, "It doesn't matter what job you have or what career you are pursuing. The people who are happy in what they do have a different way of looking at their work. They see their life's work as an offering not an offering plate."

This is what Paul meant when he said that we should offer ourselves as a living sacrifice to God. Make your whole life an offering. The more you pour out, the more it gets replaced. If you make your life a collection plate where you exist just to receive, life gets confusing. Unhappy people see themselves as collection plates. Happy people see themselves as offerings. The "glad to go attitude" will help the will of God find you.

The Willing To Grow Attitude

God's will finds people who are eager to keep on growing. That is why Paul says, *"Do not conform yourselves to the standards of this world, but let God transform you inwardly by a complete change of your mind."* (Romans 12:2) Don't let the world press you into a mold where you can't grow, move, and create. Let God transform you from within by totally renewing your mind. Be glad to grow. The number one symptom of a happy person is the will to keep on growing.

You know, I'm a sucker for the circus. I love it! I put on the funny hats, I eat the cotton candy and popcorn. I love the elephants and lions. But what I really love are the trapeze acts. I'm afraid of heights. My height is about as high as I can get without getting dizzy. To watch the trapeze artists climb up there is fascinating enough. But the thing that stops my heart is when a performer is swinging back and forth with his back to the bar behind him, and he lets go in mid-air, pirouettes, and catches the unseen bar behind him. In that instant when he is suspended, my heart stops. To me, that is the greatest analogy of what it means to find God's will. You must let go of safety, and trust that God is on the other side. I prefer to hold on to one bar and wait until I can reach the other one before I let go.

I got a letter recently from an eight year old boy named Danny who was given an assignment in school to explain God. This is his explanation:

"One of God's main jobs is making people. He makes them to replace the ones who die so there will be enough people left on earth to do things. He doesn't make grown ups, just babies. I think it is because they are smaller and easier to make. That way He doesn't have to spend time teaching them to walk and talk. He can leave that to the mothers and fathers.

"God's second most important job is listening to prayers. An awful lot of this goes on. Some people, like preachers and things, pray at other times besides bedtime. God doesn't have time to listen to the radio or television on account of this. God sees everything, He hears everything, He is everywhere—which keeps Him very busy. So, you shouldn't waste His time by going over your parents' head and asking for something they said you couldn't have.

"Now Jesus is God's Son. He used to do

all the hard work, like walking on water and performing miracles and trying to teach people who didn't want to learn about God. They finally got tired of Him preaching to them, so they just crucified Him. But He was good and kind and told God that they didn't know what they were doing and to forgive them, and so God said, 'Okay.'

"*His Dad (God) appreciated everything He had done and all His hard work on earth, so He told Him that He didn't have to go on the road anymore. He could just stay in Heaven. So He did. And now He helps His Dad out by listening to prayers and taking care of things without having to bother God. He's like a secretary, except more important. Now you can pray anytime you want to and they are sure to hear you because they have things worked out so that one of them is on call all the time.*

"*You should always go to church on Sunday because it makes God happy, and if there is anybody you want to make happy it is God. Don't skip church to do something you think is more important like going to the beach. This is wrong. Besides, the sun doesn't come out at the beach until noon anyway.*

"If you don't believe in God you will be very lonely because your parents can't go everywhere with you—like to camp. But He can. It's good to know that He is around when you are scared in the dark or you can't swim very well and you get thrown into the deep water by the big kids. But you shouldn't just always think of what God can do for you. I figure God put me here and He can take me back anytime He pleases and that's why I believe in God."

"Of such is the Kingdom of Heaven." "Out of the mouth of babes comes great wisdom." Why? Because Danny's heart is open. He hasn't stopped growing. God's will finds people who are glad to keep growing.

The popular movie, *"The Apostle,"* is a story

of a stereo-typical Pentecostal evangelist who is a womanizer, drinker, and money grubber. The movie starts at the pinnacle of this preacher's career, but then his wife has an affair. The evangelist takes a pistol and wants to kill the guy but He keeps hearing the voice of God saying, *"Thou shalt not kill."*

The next time the preacher sees this man at the ball diamond, however, he hits him in the head, kills him, and then flees for his life. He makes his way to a small town in Louisiana and cons a black preacher into letting him have his little ramshackle, abandoned church. He can't completely become a scalawag, however, and all through the movie he still leaves open a little window in his heart. You see the progression of how the window gets wider and wider because he cannot shake off the calling of God. He finally ends up on a chain gang, leading the other convicts in chants about Jesus.

There is a great message in that movie: If you keep a little crack open in your heart, then God can do great things with you no matter how broken you are.

So don't go trying to find the will of God—God's will finds you...

It finds you when you are glad to know. Don't be afraid to know the will of God. What He wants for you is best for you.

It finds you when you are glad to go. But remember—He doesn't reveal Himself to tire-kickers. Peace and God's will go together.

So, go to a quiet place and simply ask God, "What do you want me to do? What do you want me to be? How can I hitch my dream to your scheme?"

Be glad to know, glad to go, and glad to grow.

ABOUT THE AUTHOR

Think of Dr. Gerald Mann as a guide for your spiritual journey into the new millennium. Dr. Mann delivers his message of common sense and hope throughout the nation. His television program, ***Real Life!*** is available weekly in over 70 million homes. His books include *Jesus, B.C., Common Sense Religion, When the Bad Times are Over for Good, When One Day at a Time is Too Long,* and *The Book of Wisecracks.*

Dr. Mann is the senior pastor of Riverbend Church in Austin, Texas. He and his wife, Lois, have three children and four grandchildren.